Australian Slangs and Expression Handbook

Unlocking Aussie Lingo for Everyday Conversations

Stephen Watkins

Table Of Content

Introduction

Understanding Australian Slang

Australian slang, often referred to as "Strine," is a vibrant and integral component of the nation's identity. Characterized by its unique expressions, abbreviations, and inventive wordplay, Australian slang reflects the country's history, values, and sense of humor. For newcomers and even some locals, these colloquialisms can be both intriguing and perplexing. Phrases like "fair dinkum" (genuine), "arvo" (afternoon), and "bush telly" (campfire) exemplify the creativity inherent in Australian English.

The origins of Australian slang are as diverse as the country itself. Influences range from the British convicts and settlers who arrived in the 18th and 19th centuries to the rich linguistic contributions of Indigenous Australians. Over time, this melting pot of cultures and experiences gave rise to a distinct vernacular that continues to evolve. Understanding this slang offers more than just the ability to decode unfamiliar terms; it provides insight into the Australian way of life, social norms, and cultural nuances.

The Evolution of Aussie Expressions

The development of Australian slang is a testament to the nation's adaptability and innovation. In the early colonial period, settlers and convicts brought with them various dialects and slang from Britain and Ireland. These linguistic elements merged with words borrowed from Indigenous languages, resulting in a unique dialect. For instance, the word "kangaroo" originates from the Guugu Yimithirr language, highlighting the integration of Indigenous terms into everyday speech.

As Australia transitioned from a penal colony to a federation, its language continued to adapt. The gold rushes of the 1850s introduced new slang terms, as did the experiences of Australian soldiers during World War I and II. The latter gave rise to expressions like "Anzac" (Australian and New Zealand Army Corps) and "digger" (soldier), which remain in use today. In the post-war era, American culture, through cinema and music, also left its mark on Australian English, introducing terms that were localized to fit the Australian context.

In contemporary times, globalization and the digital age have further influenced Australian slang. The internet, social media, and increased cultural exchange have introduced new expressions while also reviving older ones. Despite these external influences, Australians have maintained a distinctive linguistic identity, often modifying or abbreviating borrowed terms to align with their penchant for brevity and humor.

Importance of Slang in Australian Culture

Slang serves as a linguistic badge of identity for Australians, fostering a sense of belonging and camaraderie. It reflects the national ethos of egalitarianism, where informal language breaks down social barriers and promotes inclusivity. Using slang can signify membership within a group, and understanding it is often seen as a rite of passage for newcomers.

Moreover, Australian slang encapsulates the nation's humor, resilience, and resourcefulness. Expressions like "she'll be right" (everything will be okay) and "no worries" (it's all good) highlight an optimistic and laid-back attitude, while terms like "battler" (someone who perseveres through hard times) underscore the value placed on perseverance.

In literature, music, and media, Australian slang enriches storytelling by adding authenticity and depth to characters and narratives. Authors like John Blackman, in works such as Best of Aussie Slang, have compiled and celebrated these expressions, preserving them for future generations. Such works not only entertain but also educate, ensuring that the richness of Australian vernacular is recognized and appreciated both domestically and internationally.

Understanding and appreciating Australian slang is essential for anyone seeking to fully engage with the culture. It offers a window into the national psyche, revealing values, humor, and historical experiences that have shaped the Australian identity. Whether you're planning a visit, building relationships with Australians, or simply intrigued by linguistic diversity, delving into Aussie slang will enhance your appreciation of this dynamic and spirited culture.

In this handbook, we will explore the multifaceted world of Australian slang, tracing its origins, examining its evolution, and highlighting its significance in contemporary society. Through this journey, you'll gain not only a vocabulary of colorful expressions but also a deeper understanding of the Australian way of life.

Chapter 1

Everyday Expressions

Common Greetings and Farewells

Australian English is rich with informal greetings and farewells that reflect the nation's friendly and laid-back culture.

Greetings:

G'day: A quintessential Australian greeting, "G'day" is a contraction of "Good day" and is used at any time.

How ya goin'?: Equivalent to "How are you?" or "How's it going?"

G'day, mate: Combines "G'day" with "mate," a term of friendship.

Hey: A casual greeting similar to "Hi" or "Hello."

Morning/Arvo/Evening: Shortened forms of "Good morning," "Good afternoon," and "Good evening."

Farewells:

Hooroo: An informal way to say "Goodbye" or "See you later."

Catch ya later: Means "See you later."

See ya: Short for "See you later."

Ta-ta: An informal way to say "Goodbye."

Bye: A simple and universal farewell.

Conversational Phrases

Australians often use colloquial expressions in daily conversations, many of which involve abbreviations or playful language.

No worries: Means "It's okay" or "No problem."

She'll be right: Expresses confidence that a situation will turn out fine.

Fair dinkum: Means "genuine" or "honest."

True blue: Describes someone as genuinely Australian.

Flat out like a lizard drinking: Means extremely busy.

Spit the dummy: To have a tantrum or become very upset.

Carry on like a pork chop: To behave foolishly or overact.

Dog's breakfast: Something that is messy or poorly done.

Do the Harry: To disappear or leave abruptly.

Expressions of Agreement and Disagreement

Australians have unique ways of expressing agreement or disagreement, often using colorful language.

Agreement:

Too right: Means "Absolutely" or "I agree."

Spot on: Means "Exactly right."

You beauty: An exclamation of approval or excitement.

Good on ya: Means "Well done" or "I agree with you."

Righto: Means "Okay" or "I understand."

Disagreement:

Not on your nelly: Means "Absolutely not."

Pull the other one: Expresses disbelief, similar to "You're joking."

Yeah, nah: A colloquial way of saying "No."

Rack off: A dismissive way to tell someone to go away.

Fair go: A plea for fairness, often used when someone feels they're being treated unjustly.

Understanding these expressions can greatly enhance communication and help in navigating social interactions in Australia.

Chapter 2

Social and Cultural Slang

Pub and Drinking Terminology

Australia's vibrant pub culture has given rise to a rich lexicon of slang terms related to drinking and socializing. Understanding these expressions can enhance one's experience in Australian social settings.

Common Terms for Alcohol and Drinking:

Grog: A general term for alcohol, encompassing beer, wine, and spirits.

Booze: Another broad term for alcoholic beverages.

Piss: Colloquial term for beer; "on the piss" means engaging in heavy drinking.

Plonk: Refers specifically to cheap wine.

Turps: Slang for spirits or hard liquor.

Goon: Boxed wine, often inexpensive and associated with budget drinking.

Pub-Related Slang:

Bottle-O: A liquor store where one can purchase takeaway alcohol.

Boozer: A pub or bar.

Shout: To buy a round of drinks for a group; taking turns to "shout" is customary in Australian drinking culture.

Middy: A measure of beer, typically 285ml, used in New South Wales and Western Australia.

Pot: A 285ml glass of beer, commonly used in Victoria and Queensland.

Schooner: A larger beer glass, usually 425ml, prevalent in New South Wales and Queensland.

Pint: A 570ml glass of beer, standard in South Australia and gaining popularity elsewhere.

Expressions Related to Drinking:

On the piss: Engaging in a drinking session.

Bender: An extended period of heavy drinking, often lasting multiple days.

Legless: Extremely intoxicated to the point of being unable to walk.

Maggoted: Heavily drunk.

Smashed: Intoxicated.

Blotto: Completely drunk.

Dry as a dead dingo's donger: Extremely thirsty, often implying a desire for an alcoholic drink.

Hair of the dog: Consuming alcohol to alleviate a hangover.

Understanding these terms can significantly enhance social interactions in Australian pubs and bars, allowing for seamless integration into local customs and conversations.

Sports-Related Slang

Sport is integral to Australian culture, and with it comes a plethora of slang terms unique to various games. Familiarity with this terminology offers deeper insight into the nation's sporting passions.

Australian Rules Football (AFL) Slang:

Footy: Affectionate term for Australian Rules Football.

Specky: Short for "spectacular mark"; refers to an impressive aerial catch.

Screamer: Another term for a spectacular mark.

Sausage roll: Rhyming slang for a goal, often shortened to "sausage."

Behind: A one-point score, achieved by kicking the ball between a goalpost and a behind post.

Dribble kick: A low, bouncing kick aimed at scoring a goal.

Don't argue: A stiff-arm fend used to ward off opponents.

Mongrel kick: A poorly executed kick that unpredictably wobbles through the air.

Falcon: Accidentally being hit in the head by the ball.

Rugby Slang:

Footy: Also used to refer to Rugby League or Rugby Union, depending on the region.

Scrum: A method of restarting play involving players packing closely together.

Sin bin: The area where a player sits out temporarily as a penalty.

Dummy pass: A fake pass intended to deceive the opposition.

Grubber kick: A kick that makes the ball roll and bounce unpredictably along the ground.

Hospital pass: A pass that puts the receiver in a vulnerable position, likely to be tackled hard.

Meat pie: Rhyming slang for a try (scoring in rugby).

Cricket Slang:

Duck: A term used when a batsman gets out without scoring any runs. If the batsman is dismissed on the very first ball, it's called a "golden duck."

Slogger: Refers to a batsman who plays aggressively, swinging at nearly every ball to hit boundaries.

Bouncer: A short-pitched delivery bowled by a fast bowler that bounces up near the batsman's chest or head.

Yorker: A delivery aimed directly at the batsman's feet, often used to dismiss them by hitting the stumps.

All-rounder: A player proficient in both batting and bowling.

Nightwatchman: A lower-order batsman sent in late in the day to protect top-order batsmen from being dismissed.

Caught in the slips: A term for when a batsman is dismissed by being caught by one of the fielders standing close to the wicket.

Other Sporting Slang:

Barrack: To cheer or support a team enthusiastically. It's a vital part of Australian sports culture.

Umpy: A term for an umpire in any sport, often shouted out in frustration or jest during games.

Clanger: A term for a significant mistake made by a player.

Flogs: A derogatory term for a team or individuals who perform poorly.

Mad Monday: Celebrated by sports teams at the end of their season, often involving heavy partying and fun.

Understanding Australian sports slang is essential for engaging in conversations about the country's favorite pastime and experiencing the unique atmosphere at matches, where these terms come to life. They reflect not only the games themselves but the camaraderie, humor, and intense passion Australians have for their sports.

Terms of Endearment and Nicknames

Australians are known for their tendency to assign nicknames and terms of endearment to almost everyone and everything. These terms are often humorous, affectionate, or descriptive, and they form a vital part of Australian culture.

Nicknames:

Aussie Habit of Shortening Names: Australians are notorious for shortening or modifying names. For example, someone named "Michael" might become "Mick," "Steve" becomes "Stevo," and "Sharon" might be called "Shazza."

O or A Suffixes: Adding "o" or "a" to the end of names is common. For instance, "John" becomes "Johnno," and "Tom" might become "Tommo."

Rhyming Nicknames: Australians love playful nicknames based on rhyming. A person with the last name "Smith" might be called "Smithy," and someone named "Taylor" could become "Tayls."

Occupation-Based Nicknames: Nicknames often stem from someone's profession. A plumber might be called "Pipes," while a baker might be affectionately referred to as "Doughy."

Terms of Endearment:

Mate: One of the most iconic Australian terms, "mate" is used to address friends and even strangers in a friendly way.

Love/Darl: Commonly used, especially in rural or casual settings, to address someone affectionately, such as a friend, partner, or even a customer.

Cobber: An old-fashioned term of endearment meaning a close friend, still occasionally used in some regions.

Legend: Used to compliment someone who has done something remarkable or helpful.

Chook: A playful and affectionate term, often used to refer to a woman or partner, derived from the Australian word for "chicken."

Descriptive Nicknames and Slang:

Australians also assign nicknames based on distinctive traits, habits, or even physical characteristics.

Bluey: Ironically used for someone with red hair.

Slim: Often given to someone who is not slim at all, as a playful contradiction.

Curly: A nickname for someone with very curly or, humorously, no hair at all.

Snowy: Typically used for someone with pale skin or blond hair.

Big Fella/Little Fella: Descriptive nicknames that refer to someone's size.

Cultural Importance of Terms of Endearment:

These nicknames and terms serve as more than just playful monikers; they are indicative of the egalitarian and friendly nature of Australian society. Using such terms breaks down barriers, creates a sense of belonging, and adds warmth to social interactions. Whether you're at a barbecue, the workplace, or a sports event, you're likely to encounter these affectionate expressions, making them a cornerstone of Aussie communication.

Mastering these social and cultural slang terms can provide a deeper connection to Australian culture. These phrases not only enrich the vocabulary but also offer a glimpse into the humor, camaraderie, and traditions that make Australian society unique.

Chapter 3

Workplace and Trade Slang

Australian workplaces are rich with unique slang and jargon that reflect the nation's culture, humor, and approach to work. Understanding these terms is essential for effective communication and integration into various professional environments across Australia.

Office Jargon

In Australian offices, a blend of colloquialisms and corporate jargon creates a distinctive communication style. Familiarity with these expressions can enhance workplace interactions and help in navigating daily tasks.

Arvo: Short for 'afternoon'. For example, "Let's schedule the meeting for this arvo."

Cuppa: Refers to a cup of tea or coffee. For instance, "I'm going to grab a cuppa; would you like one?"

Bludger: A term for someone who is lazy or avoids work. For example, "Don't be a bludger; finish your report on time."

Chock-a-block: Means full or crowded. For instance, "The conference room is chock-a-block with equipment."

Chook: An affectionate term for a woman; also means chicken. For example, "Thanks for your help, chook."

Chuck a sickie: To take a day off work by pretending to be sick. For instance, "I might chuck a sickie tomorrow and go to the beach."

Dag: Refers to someone who is unfashionable or socially awkward, often used affectionately. For example, "He's such a dag, but we love him."

Deadset: Means absolutely or seriously. For instance, "Are you deadset about finishing the project by Friday?"

Get your ducks in a row: To get organized. For example, "Before the presentation, make sure you get your ducks in a row."

Circle back: To revisit a topic or issue later. For instance, "Let's circle back to this discussion after lunch."

Think outside the box: To think creatively. For example, "We need to think outside the box to solve this problem."

Touch base: To make contact or reconnect. For instance, "I'll touch base with you next week about the project status."

At the end of the day: Means when everything is taken into consideration. For example, "At the end of the day, client satisfaction is what matters."

Raincheck: To reschedule plans. For instance, "I can't make it today; can we take a raincheck on our meeting?"

No worries: Means no problem or it's okay. For example, "Thanks for your help." "No worries!"

Flat out: Extremely busy. For instance, "I've been flat out all week preparing for the conference."

Smoko: A short break, traditionally for smoking but now refers to any break. For example, "I'm heading out for a smoko; be back in 10."

Bring a plate: An invitation to contribute food to a gathering. For instance, "We're having a team lunch; please bring a plate."

Fair go: A reasonable opportunity. For example, "Everyone deserves a fair go at the promotion."

Hard yakka: Hard work. For instance, "Completing the project ahead of schedule took some hard yakka."

Stickybeak: A nosy person. For example, "Don't be a stickybeak; respect their privacy."

Have a yarn: To have a chat. For instance, "Let's have a yarn about the new marketing strategy."

Good on ya: Well done or good for you. For example, "You closed the deal? Good on ya!"

She'll be right: It will be okay. For instance, "Facing a tight deadline, but she'll be right."

Spit the dummy: To throw a tantrum. For example, "The client spat the dummy over the revised proposal."

Have a crack: To attempt something. For instance, "I'll have a crack at drafting the report."

Pull your weight: To do your fair share of work. For example, "We need everyone to pull their weight on this project."

On the same page: In agreement or understanding. For instance, "Before we proceed, let's ensure we're all on the same page."

Wrap one's head around: To understand something complex. For example, "I'm still trying to wrap my head around the new software update."

Bite the bullet: To face a difficult situation bravely. For instance, "We'll have to bite the bullet and implement the changes."

Trade and Industry Terms

Trade and industry are vital to Australia's economy, and they bring with them a rich set of slang expressions and terminology. These terms often stem from the physical nature of the work, unique tools, or the camaraderie that develops in hands-on trades. Understanding this jargon is essential for effective communication in these professions, particularly for new workers or outsiders.

Construction and Building Trades Slang:

Chippy: A carpenter. For example, "The chippy is working on the framework for the new house."

Bricky: A bricklayer. "The bricky's done a great job on the retaining wall."

Sparky: An electrician. "We'll need the sparky to wire this place up before we move in."

Tradie: A tradesperson in general. "The tradies are on-site by 7 AM every morning."

Scaffoldy: A scaffolder. "The scaffoldy will set up the platforms for the painting crew."

Muso: A musician, often applied to those who perform at construction or trade events for entertainment.

Knock off: To finish work for the day. "Let's knock off early and grab a beer."

Tools down: A declaration to stop work, often used when taking a break or ending the day. "It's tools down for lunch at noon."

Dog's breakfast: Refers to a poorly done or messy job. "This wall looks like a dog's breakfast; we'll need to redo it."

Crib room: The break room or lunchroom on a construction site. "I'll meet you in the crib room for smoko."

Mining and Resource Industry Slang:

Australia's mining and resources sectors also boast a unique set of terms, reflecting the rugged and isolated environments in which many of these workers operate.

FIFO: Fly-in-fly-out, a work arrangement where employees are flown to remote job sites for shifts. "He's a FIFO worker up in the Pilbara."

Rigs: Refers to mining equipment or machinery. "The rigs need maintenance before the next shift."

Hard hat area: A safety term indicating a zone where workers must wear hard hats. "Don't enter the hard hat area without your gear."

Pit: A mining site or quarry. "The pit supervisor will give you your assignments."

Boomer: A large piece of mining equipment, or sometimes refers to an experienced worker. "The boomer operator is one of the best in the field."

Blasting: The controlled detonation of explosives in mining. "Blasting is scheduled for 3 PM, so clear the area."

Shut down: A scheduled stoppage for equipment maintenance. "There's a plant shut down next week for upgrades."

Agricultural and Farming Slang:

The agricultural industry has its own vocabulary that reflects the rural and practical nature of life on the land.

Jackaroo/Jillaroo: A male or female apprentice or worker on a cattle or sheep station. "The jackaroo is learning to muster the sheep."

Swag: A rolled-up bed used for sleeping outdoors. "I always keep a swag in the ute for long trips."

Ute: A utility vehicle, indispensable for farm work. "The ute is loaded with hay bales for the cattle."

Crutching: The process of removing wool from the rear end of sheep to prevent flystrike. "Crutching season is in full swing."

Mob: Refers to a group of livestock, especially sheep or cattle. "There's a mob of sheep in the north paddock."

On the land: A phrase used to describe working or living in agriculture. "My family has been on the land for generations."

Cockie: A farmer, especially one who raises livestock. "The cockies are facing a tough drought this year."

Hospitality and Retail Slang:

Australia's hospitality and retail industries also have their own unique expressions that workers and customers frequently use.

Barbie: Short for barbecue, an essential part of Australian hospitality. "We'll fire up the barbie for the dinner rush."

Counter meal: A meal served at a pub or bar. "The counter meal here is famous for its schnitzels."

Bottle-o: A liquor store. "Grab some beers from the bottle-o on your way home."

Flat out: Extremely busy. "We've been flat out since the lunch crowd came in."

Till: The cash register. "I'll need to count the till before the end of the shift."

Military and Emergency Services Slang

The Australian military, police, and emergency services are communities steeped in tradition, camaraderie, and unique terminology. These expressions are often used to communicate quickly and effectively in high-pressure situations.

Military Slang:

Diggers: A term for Australian soldiers, originally used during World War I. "The diggers were honored at the ANZAC Day ceremony."

Nasho: Refers to someone completing national service. "Back in the day, my grandfather was a Nasho."

Drongo: A derogatory term for someone perceived as foolish or inept. "Don't be a drongo; follow the protocol."

Civvy Street: Civilian life, as opposed to military service. "After 20 years in the Army, adjusting to Civvy Street can be tough."

Mess: The dining hall or communal eating area. "The mess serves breakfast at 0600 hours."

Skippy badge: Slang for the emblem worn by Australian Army personnel. "He proudly wears his Skippy badge on his uniform."

Emergency Services Slang:

Ambo: A paramedic or ambulance driver. "The ambo was quick to arrive at the scene of the accident."

Firies: Firefighters. "The firies did a fantastic job containing the bushfire."

Coppers: Police officers. "The coppers arrived just in time to break up the fight."

SES: State Emergency Service volunteers who respond to natural disasters. "The SES helped sandbag the town during the floods."

MICA: Mobile Intensive Care Ambulance paramedics specializing in advanced medical care. "The MICA team stabilized the patient before transport."

Jaws of life: Hydraulic tools used by emergency responders to free trapped individuals. "The jaws of life were used to rescue the driver from the wreckage."

Code brown: A term used in hospitals and emergency services to indicate a hazardous materials incident. "The hospital declared a code brown after the chemical spill."

The Role of Slang in Workplace and Trade Environments

Workplace and trade slang serve several purposes, from fostering camaraderie and team spirit to streamlining communication in high-stress situations. These terms reflect the practical, no-nonsense attitudes often found in Australian workplaces. They also reinforce a sense of belonging and shared identity among workers, whether on a construction site, in an office, or on the front lines of emergency services.

Understanding and using these terms correctly is essential for anyone looking to navigate Australian workplaces effectively. They not only enhance communication but also offer insight into the humor, practicality, and unique character of the Australian work environment.

Chapter 4

Regional Variations

Australia is a vast and diverse country, and this diversity is reflected in the regional variations of its slang. While many expressions are understood across the nation, some slang terms are unique to specific states or regions. These differences provide valuable insight into the cultural, historical, and social fabric of Australia. In addition, Indigenous influences and the divide between urban and rural lifestyles have further shaped the language, creating a vibrant tapestry of expressions that are both distinctly Australian and regionally nuanced.

Slang from Different Australian States

Each Australian state has developed its own slang vocabulary, influenced by its history, demographics, and local culture. These differences make it possible to identify where someone is from based on the expressions they use.

In New South Wales, for example, some expressions are tied to the state's vibrant beach culture. The term "Esky," referring to a portable cooler, is commonly used by beachgoers. Sydney's multicultural population has also influenced the local vernacular, with words borrowed from various immigrant communities becoming part of the everyday slang.

Victoria, home to Melbourne, is known for its coffee culture, and this is reflected in the language. Terms like "brekkie" (breakfast) and "smashed avo" (smashed avocado) are common in cafes across the state. Victorians also refer to soft drinks as "softies," and they have a habit of shortening words, giving the language a laid-back feel.

Queensland, often referred to as the "Sunshine State," has its own unique set of slang terms influenced by its tropical climate and laid-back lifestyle. The term "togs," for example, is used to describe swimwear, while "arvo" is frequently used for afternoon. Queenslanders also have a reputation for being particularly friendly, and their slang reflects this with casual, relaxed expressions.

South Australia is notable for some linguistic quirks, including its preference for the term "fruchocs" to describe a popular local confectionery. The state's unique take on food culture is also reflected in expressions like "Fritz," which refers to a type of deli meat, known elsewhere in Australia as "devon" or "polony."

Western Australia, with its vast landscapes and isolation from the rest of the country, has developed its own distinct slang. Terms like "seabreeze" (referring to a specific wind pattern that cools the Perth coastline) and "quokka selfie" (a photo with the iconic Rottnest Island marsupial) have emerged in recent years. The state's love of outdoor activities also leads to phrases like "sundowner," used to describe drinks at sunset.

Tasmania, Australia's island state, is rich in terms related to its natural environment. Locals often use words like "tassie" to describe their state, and phrases like "the apple isle" reflect its historical connection to apple farming. Fishing and outdoor activities dominate the culture, with expressions like "going for a flick" (fishing with a rod) being common.

The Northern Territory, with its rugged outback lifestyle and large Indigenous population, has slang that reflects both its geography and cultural diversity. The term "bush tucker" (referring to native Australian food) is widely used, as are phrases like "top end" (referring to the northernmost part of the territory) and "dry season" (used to describe the cooler months).

The Australian Capital Territory (ACT), being the political center of the country, often borrows slang from other states but has a few unique terms tied to its government-centric lifestyle. Expressions like "pollies" (politicians) and "Canberran" (a resident of Canberra) are frequently used.

Indigenous Influences on Australian Slang

Australia's Aboriginal and Torres Strait Islander peoples have had a profound impact on the country's language, including its slang. Indigenous words and phrases have been adopted into Australian English, reflecting the deep connection between the land, its First Nations people, and their cultural heritage.

One of the most notable contributions is the use of Indigenous place names. Many towns, rivers, and landmarks retain their traditional names, such as "Kakadu," "Woolloomooloo," and "Kununurra." These words often carry significant cultural and historical meaning, providing a window into the traditions and stories of the land's original inhabitants.

Everyday slang has also been enriched by Indigenous languages. Words like "yakka" (hard work), "bung" (broken), and "cooee" (a call used to attract attention) have roots in Aboriginal languages and are now widely understood across Australia. "Yakka," for instance, comes from the Yagara language of Queensland and is commonly used in workplaces to describe effort or toil.

Indigenous food terms have also become a part of Australian slang. "Bush tucker," as mentioned earlier, encompasses traditional Aboriginal foods such as kangaroo, emu, and native plants like wattleseed and bush tomatoes. These terms highlight the close relationship between Aboriginal culture and the natural environment.

Another significant influence is seen in the names of animals and plants. Words like "kangaroo," "koala," "dingo," and "billabong" are derived from Indigenous languages and are now integral to the Australian lexicon. These words not only describe unique elements of the Australian landscape but also serve as a reminder of the country's Indigenous heritage.

Indigenous storytelling traditions have also inspired expressions that reflect connection to land and community. Phrases like "walkabout," which originally referred to a spiritual journey on foot, have entered common usage, although sometimes in ways that stray from their original meaning.

The influence of Indigenous languages on Australian slang is a testament to the resilience and richness of Aboriginal culture. As awareness of Australia's First Nations people continues to grow, there is a renewed effort to preserve and celebrate these contributions to the country's language.

Urban vs. Rural Expressions

The divide between urban and rural Australia is another factor that influences the country's slang. While urban centers like Sydney, Melbourne, and Brisbane are hubs of multiculturalism and innovation, rural areas—often referred to as "the bush" or "the outback"—are characterized by a more traditional, down-to-earth lifestyle. This distinction is reflected in the language used by people in these regions.

In urban areas, slang tends to be fast-evolving and influenced by global trends. Younger generations in cities often adopt terms from pop culture, technology, and social media, creating a dynamic and ever-changing vocabulary. Expressions like "lit," "ghosting," and "sliding into DMs" are just as common in Australian cities as they are in other parts of the English-speaking world.

City slang is also shaped by multiculturalism. With large immigrant populations, urban centers incorporate words and phrases from a variety of languages. For example, terms like "bao" (a type of Chinese steamed bun) and "mezze" (a selection of small dishes from Middle Eastern cuisine) are frequently used in urban food culture. This fusion of languages and cultures gives urban slang a global and inclusive feel.

In contrast, rural slang reflects the slower pace and practical nature of life in the bush. Words and phrases are often tied to farming, wildlife, and outdoor activities. For example, "fair dinkum" (genuine or honest) is a quintessentially rural expression, as is "swagman," which refers to a laborer who travels on foot with a bedroll. These terms evoke images of Australia's outback and its traditional way of life.

Rural slang also includes a wealth of colorful expressions that highlight the humor and resourcefulness of country life. Phrases like "flat out like a lizard drinking" (extremely busy) and "he's got a few roos loose in the top paddock" (a playful way of saying someone is eccentric) are examples of the wit and creativity found in rural language.

The divide between urban and rural expressions is not just geographical but also cultural. While urban slang is influenced by modernity and globalization, rural slang remains deeply connected to Australia's heritage and the land. Both forms of expression, however, are essential to understanding the full spectrum of Australian language and culture.

The regional variations in Australian slang reflect the country's diversity, history, and unique way of life. From state-specific terms to Indigenous influences and the urban-rural divide, these expressions capture the essence of what it means to be Australian. By exploring and understanding these regional differences, one gains a deeper appreciation for the rich and multifaceted nature of Australia's language.

Chapter 5

Rhyming Slang and Diminutives

Australian English is renowned for its rich use of creative language, and among the most distinctive features of this dialect are its rhyming slang and diminutives. These linguistic quirks add color and character to everyday conversations, and their origins reflect both the history of the Australian people and their unique approach to communication. This chapter delves into the intricacies of rhyming slang and diminutives, two features of Australian English that not only distinguish it from other forms of English but also showcase the creativity and humor that define the Australian identity.

Understanding Rhyming Slang

Rhyming slang, a beloved feature of Australian English, is a playful and inventive way of speaking that involves replacing a word with a phrase that rhymes with the intended word. The rhyme itself often makes sense in the context of the conversation, but the real trick of rhyming slang is that, after the phrase is used, speakers often omit the rhyming word, leaving the non-rhyming word as the actual term. This twist on language creates an additional layer of humor and challenge for those not familiar with the slang.

The roots of rhyming slang can be traced back to the 19th century in the working-class districts of London, particularly in the Cockney dialect. Early Australian settlers, particularly from London, brought this form of slang with them, where it evolved and integrated with the broader Australian vernacular. As a result, Australian rhyming slang carries the influence of Cockney rhyming slang but with a distinctly Aussie flair.

A classic example of Australian rhyming slang is "apples and pears," which rhymes with "stairs." In normal conversation, this phrase would be shortened to just "apples." So, when an Australian says, "I'm going up the apples," they mean they're heading upstairs. The rhyme is cleverly concealed, which is part of the fun for those in the know.

Another widely recognized example is "dog and bone," which rhymes with "phone." In typical usage, the phrase would be reduced to just "dog." If an Australian says, "I'll just grab the dog," they are referring to picking up the phone. Similarly, "bread and honey" is used for "money," though in conversation, it might be shortened to simply "bread."

Rhyming slang often incorporates Australian culture, humor, and even local events. For instance, "Captain Cook" is a rhyming phrase for "look." In everyday conversation, Australians might say, "Give us a Captain Cook at that," meaning, "Take a look at that." While the original rhyme seems straightforward, the way it is used in casual speech shows how rhyming slang has become embedded in Australian expressions.

In addition to its role as a humorous linguistic device, rhyming slang has an almost secretive quality. In the past, it was often used as a way for people in certain social classes—such as criminals or tradespeople—to communicate with each other without outsiders understanding. The rhyming element, particularly when the rhyming word is dropped, gives those using the slang a form of linguistic camouflage.

While rhyming slang may seem to be a quirky and outdated form of expression, it remains a beloved and important part of Australian identity. It is particularly common in the working-class areas, and its use has been passed down through generations. In the modern context, Australians often use rhyming slang in casual conversation or in settings where humor and camaraderie are central.

However, as with any form of slang, the use of rhyming expressions has been slowly fading in mainstream speech. Younger Australians may not be as familiar with the traditional rhyming phrases as their older counterparts, though many still remain in popular culture and everyday language. Rhyming slang, in its authentic form, is perhaps one of the most cherished aspects of Australia's linguistic heritage.

Common Diminutives in Australian English

Diminutives are another hallmark of Australian English. These shortened versions of words, often with an affectionate or informal tone, reflect the relaxed and friendly nature of Australian culture. The creation of diminutives in Australia is a product of the nation's love for informal language and its tendency to shorten and simplify words for convenience and ease of communication.

In Australian English, diminutives are formed by taking a word and then shortening it, often by adding a vowel sound at the end of the word. The most common diminutive suffix is "-o" or "-ie," although other variations exist. Diminutives are widely used in both formal and informal conversations, and they serve to make language more personal, approachable, and less stiff or formal. Some words, when shortened into diminutives, even take on new meanings or cultural connotations.

One of the most common diminutives in Australian English is the word "arvo," a shortened form of "afternoon." Australians frequently use "arvo" in casual conversation, such as when someone says, "I'll see you this arvo" to mean, "I'll see you this afternoon." This informal, friendly form of expression helps to establish rapport and convey a sense of relaxation and ease.

Similarly, "bottle-o" is a diminutive of "bottle shop," which refers to a store where alcohol is sold. Australians will often say, "I'm heading to the bottle-o" when they plan to buy some drinks. Similarly, "servo" is a commonly used diminutive for "service station," which refers to a gas station or petrol station. "I'll stop at the servo" means "I'll stop at the service station."

Other common diminutives include "chook," a term for chicken, which can be used both for the bird and for chicken meat. If someone says, "I'm having chook for dinner," they mean they are having chicken for dinner. "Sunnies" is the diminutive for "sunglasses," and Australians will often say, "Don't forget your sunnies" when reminding someone to bring their sunglasses.

"Doll" is often used as a diminutive for "doll face," referring to a woman, though it can be used affectionately for children, too. "Cuppa," meaning "cup of tea" or "coffee," is another popular diminutive, and it's used frequently in Australian English, such as in the sentence, "Let's have a cuppa." The word "footy," short for "football," is also extremely popular in Australia, and the term is used widely to refer to the sport, particularly Australian Rules football. "I'm going to the footy this weekend" means, "I'm going to watch a football game this weekend."

In addition to these examples, Australian diminutives are often formed from local names or places. For example, "Melbs" is a common short form of Melbourne, and "Brisvegas" is a playful diminutive for Brisbane. These shortened terms show the easygoing nature of Australian speech and often add a sense of humor to conversations.

Australian diminutives are not only limited to nouns; they also appear in adjectives and adverbs. For instance, "smoko" is a diminutive of "smoke break" and refers to a short break, often taken during work hours. In a work setting, someone might say, "It's time for a smoko" to indicate it's time to take a break. "Maccas," referring to McDonald's, is another example of a diminutive that's widely used in Australia.

The use of diminutives in Australian English creates an intimate and friendly atmosphere. It is part of the Australian spirit of casualness, making interactions feel less formal and more personal. Whether among friends, family, or colleagues, diminutives make conversations feel warmer and more approachable. It is also a way of showing affection, as many diminutives have a tone of endearment. This is especially true for terms like "bub" (short for baby) or "mate" (a term for a friend or companion).

Moreover, diminutives serve as a form of linguistic efficiency. Australians have a reputation for speaking quickly and using shorthand, and diminutives help make communication more efficient. Whether talking about everyday objects, places, or people, Australians prefer shorter, snappier words that are easy to say and remember.

Diminutives are so ingrained in Australian culture that they are often used with a sense of pride. When foreigners hear Australians casually referring to things like "footy," "chook," and "servo," it's clear that these expressions form an integral part of the Australian identity. They reflect the country's laid-back, approachable culture and contribute to a distinct linguistic style that sets Australian English apart from other varieties of English.

Chapter 6

Humor and Insults

Australian culture is often defined by its irreverent sense of humor, characterized by an ability to find lightness and laughter even in the most mundane or challenging circumstances. Humor is deeply ingrained in Australian identity and plays a significant role in how Australians communicate, bond, and relate to one another. Central to this humor is a unique blend of playful teasing, friendly insults, and slang that permeates everything from casual conversations to stand-up comedy. This chapter explores how these elements of humor are used as social tools, reflecting Australia's values of equality, informality, and camaraderie.

Playful Teasing and Banter

Playful teasing, or "taking the mickey," is a cornerstone of Australian communication. It is a way for Australians to show affection, establish rapport, and create a sense of camaraderie. While teasing might seem offensive to outsiders, in Australian culture, it is often a sign of respect or acceptance. To be teased by an Australian is frequently an indicator that you've been welcomed into the fold.

This form of humor often involves poking fun at someone's quirks, habits, or minor mistakes in a good-natured way. For example, if someone spills a drink, they might be called "a bit of a drongo," a lighthearted term suggesting they're a bit clumsy. Such teasing is rarely meant to be hurtful and is instead a way to diffuse tension or make a situation more enjoyable.

Australians also use teasing to keep egos in check, as humility is highly valued in the culture. If someone appears to be bragging, they might be subjected to playful ribbing to remind them not to take themselves too seriously. For instance, a person boasting about their achievements might hear, "Don't strain your arm patting yourself on the back, mate." This type of banter reinforces the Australian ethos of egalitarianism, where no one is allowed to feel superior to others.

Banter is also a key component of Australian workplaces and social gatherings. It serves to break the ice, build relationships, and foster a relaxed atmosphere. For example, colleagues might tease one another about their performance during a sporting event or their inability to resist a second helping of dessert at lunch. In these situations, the humor creates a sense of inclusivity and belonging.

Sports are a particularly rich arena for playful teasing and banter in Australia. Whether it's cricket, rugby, or Australian Rules football, Australians often engage in friendly jabs about rival teams or players. Supporters of opposing teams might exchange humorous insults, such as calling one another "bandwagoners" or "tragics," all in good fun. This lighthearted rivalry helps to strengthen bonds among fans while celebrating the communal nature of sport.

It's important to note that playful teasing and banter rely on mutual understanding and context. For teasing to be effective and appreciated, it must be delivered with the right tone and intent. Australians are adept at reading social cues and ensuring their humor is appropriate for the situation and the audience. When done well, playful teasing fosters trust and connection, making it one of the most cherished aspects of Australian humor.

Friendly Insults and Their Meanings

Friendly insults, often referred to as "sledging" in Australian slang, are an extension of playful teasing. These insults are rarely meant to offend; instead, they are a way for Australians to show affection or camaraderie. Unlike malicious insults, which aim to hurt or belittle, friendly insults are delivered with a wink and a smile, signaling that no harm is intended.

A common feature of Australian-friendly insults is their use of colorful language and creative expressions. For example, someone who is acting a bit foolish might be called "a few sausages short of a barbecue" or "not the sharpest tool in the shed." These phrases are humorous ways of suggesting someone might not be thinking clearly, but they're rarely taken seriously.

Another popular friendly insult is "bogan," which refers to someone perceived as unsophisticated or unrefined. While "bogan" might sound offensive to outsiders, many Australians embrace the term with pride, seeing it as a badge of authenticity or connection to working-class roots. It's not uncommon for someone to jokingly call their friend a "bogan" for wearing thongs (flip-flops) to a fancy event or for drinking cheap beer.

Australians also use animal metaphors as friendly insults, adding a layer of humor to their interactions. For instance, calling someone a "galah" (a noisy and silly bird) suggests they're being a bit foolish or talkative. Similarly, referring to someone as a "wombat" (an animal known for its slow pace) might imply they're being lazy or slow to act.

Friendly insults are particularly common among close friends and family members, where there is an established level of trust and understanding. A sibling might call their brother or sister "a bit of a tosser" for making a questionable fashion choice, or a mate might jokingly refer to their friend as "a useless drongo" for being late to a gathering. In these cases, the insults are delivered with affection and often accompanied by laughter.

Workplaces are another setting where friendly insults thrive, particularly in male-dominated industries like construction or mining. Colleagues might refer to each other with nicknames like "old mate" or "big fella" while delivering lighthearted jabs about their work performance. These exchanges help to create a sense of camaraderie and mutual respect, reinforcing the egalitarian values that are central to Australian culture.

The success of friendly insults depends on the context and the relationship between the individuals involved. Australians are skilled at gauging when and how to use these expressions, ensuring they're taken in the spirit of fun. For outsiders, understanding the intent behind these insults is key to appreciating their humor and participating in the banter.

Slang in Australian Comedy

Slang is a vital ingredient in Australian comedy, serving as a powerful tool for creating humor that resonates with local audiences. Comedians often draw on the rich tapestry of Australian slang to craft jokes that are uniquely relatable, capturing the quirks and idiosyncrasies of everyday life in Australia.

One of the reasons slang is so effective in comedy is its ability to evoke a sense of place and identity. Words and phrases like "strewth" (an exclamation of surprise), "fair dinkum" (genuine), and "bludger" (a lazy person) are instantly recognizable to Australians and often elicit laughter through their sheer familiarity. These terms also carry cultural connotations, making them a shortcut for setting the scene or establishing a character.

Australian comedians frequently use slang to satirize aspects of the country's culture, such as its obsession with sport, love of drinking, or relaxed attitude toward life. For example, a comedian might joke about a "bloke" who spends all day at the "pub" (bar) with his "mates" (friends), painting a humorous picture of the stereotypical Aussie male. These jokes often exaggerate cultural traits for comedic effect, allowing audiences to laugh at themselves and their shared experiences.

In addition to traditional slang, comedians often invent new expressions or play with existing ones to create fresh and unexpected humor. For example, they might combine two unrelated slang terms to form a new phrase or use a well-known expression in an unusual context. This creative use of language keeps the humor dynamic and engaging, ensuring that audiences are always entertained.

Slang also plays a crucial role in the delivery of jokes, adding rhythm, tone, and authenticity to the performance. Australian comedians are known for their distinctive accents and colloquial speech patterns, which amplify the humor of their material. Phrases like "onya" (short for "good on you") or "reckon" (believe or think) are often used to punctuate jokes, making them feel more natural and conversational.

Television and film have also embraced Australian slang as a comedic device. Iconic characters like Crocodile Dundee and Kath & Kim have become synonymous with their use of exaggerated Australian expressions, delighting audiences both at home and abroad. These portrayals often celebrate the uniqueness of Australian language and humor while poking fun at cultural stereotypes.

The use of slang in Australian comedy is not limited to professional performers; it is also a staple of everyday humor among Australians themselves. Friends, family members, and colleagues often incorporate slang into their jokes and stories, using language as a way to bond and share laughter. Whether it's a witty remark, a clever pun, or a cheeky observation, slang is an integral part of how Australians express their humor.

Slang in Australian comedy highlights the country's ability to laugh at itself and find joy in the little things. It reflects the resilience, creativity, and laid-back attitude that define Australian culture, making it a source of pride and connection for audiences everywhere.

Chapter 7

Modern Slang and Internet Speak

Language is constantly evolving, and Australian slang is no exception. In today's fast-paced, digitally connected world, modern slang and internet speak have become integral to communication. From text messages to social media platforms, these contemporary expressions reflect the dynamic nature of language and the impact of technology, global trends, and pop culture on how Australians communicate. This chapter explores the latest additions to the Australian lexicon, the role of social media in shaping modern slang, and how popular culture continues to influence the way people speak.

Contemporary Expressions

Contemporary Australian slang captures the zeitgeist of modern life, incorporating new words and phrases that reflect current experiences, attitudes, and cultural phenomena. These expressions often emerge organically from specific communities or events before spreading widely through conversation, media, and digital platforms. In many cases, they blend traditional Australian slang with global influences, creating a unique hybrid that resonates with today's multicultural society.

One prominent trend in contemporary slang is the shortening or abbreviation of words, a hallmark of Australian English. Terms like "tradie" (tradesperson), "selfie" (self-portrait photograph), and "sesh" (session) have become part of everyday speech, reflecting Australians' preference for informal and efficient communication. These terms are not only easy to say but also convey a sense of camaraderie and familiarity, making them especially popular among younger generations.

Another feature of modern slang is the use of humor and irony. Australians have long been known for their irreverent sense of humor, and this trait is evident in contemporary expressions. For example, the phrase "yeah, nah" is a quintessentially Australian way of expressing polite disagreement or hesitation, while "nah, yeah" is used to affirm something. These contradictory phrases are delivered with a playful tone, adding an element of humor to even the simplest interactions.

The influence of global internet culture is also apparent in contemporary Australian slang. Terms like "vibe" (atmosphere or mood), "stan" (an obsessive fan, derived from Eminem's song of the same name), and "ghost" (to cut off communication abruptly) have been adopted from international English and seamlessly integrated into Australian vernacular. While these expressions may not have originated in Australia, their usage often takes on a distinctly local flavor, with Australians adding their own spin to the terms.

Environmental and social issues have also shaped modern slang. As Australians increasingly engage with topics like climate change and sustainability, new words and phrases have emerged to reflect these concerns. For instance, "greenie" refers to someone passionate about environmental causes, while "climate warrior" is used to describe activists advocating for change. These expressions highlight how language evolves in response to societal values and priorities.

Contemporary slang also reflects the changing dynamics of Australian identity, particularly in terms of multiculturalism and inclusivity. Words and phrases borrowed from Indigenous languages, migrant communities, and international pop culture are now common in Australian English, enriching the lexicon and broadening its cultural scope. This blending of influences demonstrates how language serves as a bridge between diverse communities, fostering understanding and connection.

Slang in Social Media

The rise of social media has had a profound impact on language, transforming how Australians communicate and giving rise to a new form of slang that is fast, creative, and ever-changing. Platforms like Instagram, TikTok, Twitter, and Snapchat serve as incubators for linguistic innovation, where trends spread rapidly and words take on new meanings almost overnight.

One of the defining characteristics of social media slang is its brevity. With character limits on platforms like Twitter and the fast-paced nature of digital interactions, users have developed a shorthand that allows them to communicate efficiently. Abbreviations like "TBH" (to be honest), "IRL" (in real life), and "BRB" (be right back) are ubiquitous in online conversations. Emojis, GIFs, and hashtags further enhance this shorthand, providing visual and symbolic elements that convey meaning without the need for lengthy explanations.

Australian social media users have adapted these global trends while infusing them with local flavor. Hashtags like #Straya (a playful abbreviation of "Australia") and #AussieLife celebrate Australian culture and humor, often accompanied by memes or images that highlight uniquely Australian experiences. Slang terms like "Avo" (avocado), "Brekkie" (breakfast), and "Sunnies" (sunglasses) frequently appear in captions and comments, reinforcing their role as staples of the Australian vernacular.

Social media also amplifies the spread of slang by creating a space for collaboration and experimentation. TikTok, for example, has become a hub for viral trends and catchphrases, where users remix and reinterpret language in creative ways. An Australian TikToker might coin a phrase that quickly gains traction, becoming part of the broader cultural lexicon. Similarly, Instagram captions and Twitter threads often serve as testing grounds for new expressions, allowing slang to evolve in real-time.

Another key feature of social media slang is its ability to create in-groups and foster a sense of community. By using specific terms or phrases, individuals can signal their affiliation with certain subcultures, interests, or values. For example, fans of Australian Rules Football might use terms like "specky" (a spectacular mark) or "footy" (football) in their posts, while food enthusiasts might reference "Aussie classics" like Vegemite or Tim Tams. This linguistic shorthand helps users connect with like-minded individuals and participate in shared cultural narratives.

However, the ephemeral nature of social media slang means that many expressions have a short lifespan. Trends come and go quickly, and words that are popular one year may fade into obscurity the next. This constant evolution reflects the fast-paced environment of social media, where creativity and novelty are prized. For Australians, keeping up with these changes can be both a challenge and a source of enjoyment, as they navigate the ever-shifting landscape of online communication.

Influence of Pop Culture on Language

Pop culture has always played a significant role in shaping language, and in Australia, its influence is particularly pronounced. Television shows, movies, music, and other forms of entertainment provide a rich source of inspiration for slang, introducing new words and phrases that capture the imagination of audiences.

Australian pop culture itself has contributed iconic expressions to the national lexicon. From classic television characters like Kath & Kim to beloved films like The Castle, these works often highlight the quirks of Australian speech, celebrating its humor and distinctiveness. Phrases like "Noice" (nice), "Look at moi" (look at me), and "Tell him he's dreamin'" have become cultural touchstones, used both humorously and affectionately in everyday conversations.

International pop culture has also left its mark on Australian slang, particularly through the influence of American and British media. Shows like Friends, The Simpsons, and Game of Thrones have popularized catchphrases and idioms that Australians have adopted and adapted. Terms like "pivot" (used humorously to indicate a change of direction, from a famous Friends scene) or "winter is coming" (a foreboding phrase from Game of Thrones) are now part of the broader cultural conversation, often used with a uniquely Australian twist.

Music and celebrity culture are additional drivers of slang evolution. Lyrics from popular songs, quotes from interviews, and viral moments on social media all contribute to the creation of new expressions. For example, Australian fans of international artists might adopt phrases from their favorite songs, blending them with local slang to create hybrid expressions. Similarly, Australian musicians and influencers often introduce new terms through their work, which then spread to their audiences.

The influence of pop culture on slang is not limited to specific words or phrases; it also extends to attitudes and ways of speaking. For instance, the rise of reality television has popularized a particular style of candid, exaggerated storytelling, which often incorporates slang and catchphrases. Viewers might emulate this style in their own conversations, adopting the tone and language they see on screen.

In addition to traditional forms of pop culture, internet memes and viral content have become powerful forces in shaping language. Memes often rely on humor, irony, and cultural references to convey their messages, introducing new expressions or repurposing existing ones. Australians are avid creators and consumers of memes, and their humor often reflects local experiences, such as encounters with wildlife, extreme weather, or uniquely Australian quirks. These memes contribute to the evolution of slang, as the language used in them becomes part of the broader cultural lexicon.

Pop culture's influence on slang underscores the dynamic relationship between language and identity. By adopting expressions from entertainment and media, Australians engage with global trends while preserving their distinct linguistic heritage. This interplay between local and global influences ensures that Australian slang remains vibrant, relevant, and ever-evolving.

Chapter 8

Slang in Australian Literature and Media

Language is one of the most powerful tools of storytelling, shaping the way stories are told and the cultural identity they convey. Australian literature and media have long been celebrated for their authentic portrayal of Australian life, and slang plays a pivotal role in this representation. By embedding slang into their narratives, authors, filmmakers, and media producers capture the essence of Australian culture, creating works that resonate deeply with local audiences while offering international audiences a glimpse into the Australian way of life. This chapter delves into the role of slang in Australian literature and media, exploring notable works, its use in film and television, and how media influences the popularity of slang.

Notable Works Featuring Aussie Slang

Australian literature has a rich history of incorporating slang to reflect the vernacular of the times and convey a strong sense of place. From early colonial writings to contemporary fiction, the use of Australian slang has provided authenticity to characters and settings, allowing readers to immerse themselves in the distinctly Australian experience.

One of the earliest examples of Australian literature featuring slang is Henry Lawson's short stories. Lawson, often referred to as the "father of Australian literature," used colloquial language and slang to portray the lives of bushmen and working-class Australians. His stories, such as The Drover's Wife and While the Billy Boils, are peppered with terms like "bushie" (bushman), "swagman" (itinerant worker), and "tucker" (food). These expressions not only lend authenticity to his characters but also highlight the resilience and humor of Australians living in harsh rural environments.

Another iconic figure in Australian literature is Banjo Paterson, whose poems capture the spirit of the Australian outback and its people. Works like The Man from Snowy River and Waltzing Matilda are filled with slang and colloquial expressions that bring the landscapes and characters to life. Phrases such as "jumbuck" (sheep) and "billabong" (a waterhole) have become synonymous with Australian culture, largely thanks to Paterson's contributions.

More contemporary examples of Australian literature continue this tradition. Authors like Tim Winton, Christos Tsiolkas, and Helen Garner frequently use slang to reflect the speech patterns of their characters and ground their stories in modern Australian settings. In Winton's Cloudstreet, for instance, characters use expressions like "bloody" (a common intensifier) and "mate" (friend) to create a sense of familiarity and intimacy. This use of slang not only makes the dialogue more realistic but also enhances the emotional depth of the story.

Australian children's literature has also embraced slang as a way to engage young readers and celebrate local culture. Books like Possum Magic by Mem Fox and the Paul Jennings series incorporate Australian expressions to introduce children to the language and traditions of their country. By using accessible and playful slang, these works foster a sense of pride in Australian identity while appealing to readers of all ages.

Analysis of Slang in Film and Television

Australian film and television have played a significant role in popularizing slang, both within the country and internationally. By incorporating colloquial language into scripts, filmmakers and showrunners create relatable characters and authentic narratives that resonate with audiences. Slang in film and television often serves as a cultural marker, highlighting the unique aspects of Australian life and humor.

One of the most iconic examples of Australian slang in film is Crocodile Dundee (1986). The character of Mick Dundee, played by Paul Hogan, embodies the archetypal Aussie larrikin, complete with a vocabulary rich in slang. Phrases like "That's not a knife, this is a knife!" and "G'day" (hello) became globally recognized, showcasing the charm and wit of Australian language. The film's success helped introduce international audiences to Australian slang, cementing its place in popular culture.

Television series like Kath & Kim have also contributed to the widespread recognition of Australian slang. The show's characters use exaggerated colloquialisms and mispronunciations, such as "noice" (nice) and "chardonnay set" (affluent individuals who enjoy white wine), to create humor and satirize suburban life. The show's clever use of language not only entertains but also provides a commentary on Australian social dynamics, making it a beloved cultural touchstone.

In Australian cinema, films like The Castle and Muriel's Wedding are renowned for their use of slang and colloquial expressions to create memorable dialogue and relatable characters. The Castle, in particular, is celebrated for its humorous depiction of a working-class Australian family, with lines like "Tell him he's dreamin'" and "How's the serenity?" becoming part of the national lexicon. These phrases capture the optimism and resilience of everyday Australians, resonating with audiences across generations.

Reality television has also embraced slang as a way to connect with viewers. Shows like MasterChef Australia and The Block often feature contestants and hosts using colloquial language, reflecting the diversity and informality of Australian speech. This use of slang helps to create an approachable and relatable atmosphere, allowing audiences to feel more connected to the participants and their stories.

Australian soap operas like Neighbours and Home and Away have had a significant impact on the spread of slang, particularly among younger audiences. These long-running shows frequently include slang in their scripts, helping to normalize its use in everyday conversation. Terms like "rego" (vehicle registration), "servo" (service station), and "arvo" (afternoon) are commonly heard in these programs, reinforcing their place in Australian vernacular.

Impact of Media on Slang Popularity

The media has a profound influence on the popularity and evolution of slang, acting as both a mirror of language trends and a catalyst for their spread. Through literature, film, television, and digital platforms, the media amplifies the use of slang, making it accessible to a wider audience and solidifying its place in the cultural lexicon.

One way media influences slang is by immortalizing certain phrases through iconic works. For example, the phrase "fair go" (a plea for fairness) gained prominence in Australian discourse partly due to its frequent use in media, where it symbolizes the nation's values of equality and opportunity. Similarly, lines from films like The Castle and Crocodile Dundee have become enduring catchphrases, ensuring their continued relevance in Australian culture.

The media also acts as a platform for introducing new slang, particularly through digital channels. Social media platforms like Instagram, TikTok, and Twitter are hotspots for linguistic innovation, where users coin and popularize new terms at a rapid pace. Australian influencers, content creators, and public figures often use slang in their posts and videos, helping to spread these expressions among their followers. The viral nature of social media ensures that slang can reach a global audience, breaking down geographical barriers and fostering a shared cultural language.

Radio and podcasts have also contributed to the dissemination of slang. Australian radio hosts and podcasters frequently use colloquial language in their shows, creating an informal and relatable atmosphere for listeners. This use of slang not only reflects contemporary speech patterns but also encourages audiences to adopt these expressions in their own conversations.

The rise of streaming platforms has further expanded the reach of Australian media and its associated slang.

International viewers of Australian shows and films on platforms like Netflix and Stan are exposed to the unique rhythms and expressions of Australian English, often adopting these terms into their own vocabularies. This global exposure helps to elevate the status of Australian slang, positioning it as an integral part of the country's cultural export.

Media representation also plays a role in preserving and promoting Indigenous Australian slang and expressions. Documentaries, films, and television programs that highlight Indigenous culture and language contribute to the broader understanding and appreciation of these linguistic traditions. By featuring Indigenous slang in their narratives, these works help to ensure that these expressions are not only preserved but also celebrated as an essential part of Australia's linguistic heritage.

The media's impact on slang is not limited to its creation and dissemination; it also influences how slang is perceived. By showcasing slang in positive and relatable contexts, the media helps to normalize its use and reduce any stigma associated with colloquial language. This shift in perception encourages individuals to embrace slang as a valid and valuable form of expression, enriching the tapestry of Australian English.

Chapter 9

Practical Application

Slang is a dynamic and integral aspect of language, offering a window into culture, identity, and social connection. However, using slang effectively requires more than just knowing the words and their meanings—it also demands an understanding of the context, tone, and appropriateness of its use. Misusing slang, even with good intentions, can lead to misunderstandings or come across as insincere. This chapter explores practical tips for using slang appropriately, the importance of understanding context and tone, and how to avoid common pitfalls to ensure clear and respectful communication.

Tips for Using Slang Appropriately

Using slang appropriately involves balancing authenticity with cultural sensitivity and awareness. While incorporating slang into conversation can enhance relatability and connection, it's important to use it thoughtfully to avoid sounding forced or out of place.

One of the most important tips for using slang effectively is to listen and observe how native speakers use it. In

Australian culture, slang often reflects shared experiences, humor, and social norms. By paying attention to how slang is used in real-life conversations, television shows, movies, or social media, you can better understand its nuances and adapt your own usage accordingly. For instance, words like "bloke" (man) or "sheila" (woman) may seem quintessentially Australian but are often used less frequently in urban areas compared to rural regions. Observing these subtleties helps prevent misuse.

It's also important to align your slang usage with your audience. For example, slang that is appropriate in casual settings, such as among friends or peers, may not be suitable in professional or formal environments. Terms like "arvo" (afternoon) or "brekkie" (breakfast) might be fine in a casual email or chat but should be avoided in a corporate meeting or formal correspondence. Understanding the social context and choosing slang that fits the situation ensures that your communication is effective and respectful.

When using slang in written communication, consider the medium and purpose. On social media or in text messages, slang can convey informality and personality. However, in professional emails, academic writing, or public presentations, excessive slang may detract from your credibility. For instance, while a phrase like "no worries" (it's okay) might work well in casual emails, it may come across as too informal in more serious contexts.

Another tip is to be mindful of regional variations and cultural connotations. Australian slang is rich and diverse, with some terms holding different meanings depending on the state or community in which they're used. For example, "thong" refers to flip-flops in Australia but means something entirely different in American English. Being aware of these differences can help you avoid potential confusion or embarrassment.

Finally, authenticity is key when using slang. Avoid overusing it or forcing it into conversation, as this can come across as insincere or inauthentic. Instead, integrate slang naturally into your speech, choosing expressions that feel comfortable and align with your personal style. If you're not confident in using a particular term, it's better to avoid it until you have a clearer understanding of its usage and context.

Understanding Context and Tone

Context and tone are critical when it comes to using slang effectively. In Australian culture, the same word or phrase can carry different meanings depending on how, when, and where it is used. Understanding these nuances ensures that your communication is both appropriate and impactful.

The social context of a conversation often dictates whether slang is suitable. In informal settings, such as a barbecue with friends or a casual chat at the pub, slang is not only acceptable but often expected. It helps create a relaxed and friendly atmosphere, fostering a sense of camaraderie. In these situations, phrases like "cheers" (thanks) or "mate" (friend) are commonplace and convey a sense of warmth and approachability.

Conversely, in formal or professional settings, the use of slang should be more restrained. While some colloquial expressions may be acceptable in relaxed workplaces or industries with a casual culture, it's generally best to err on the side of caution. For instance, while addressing colleagues as "mates" might be fine in a construction site or creative agency, it could be seen as too informal in a corporate boardroom or academic conference.

Tone also plays a significant role in determining how slang is perceived. In Australian English, tone is often conveyed through subtle shifts in intonation, delivery, and context. For example, the phrase "Yeah, right" can be used genuinely to express agreement or sarcastically to convey doubt, depending on the tone of voice. Similarly, playful insults or teasing, such as calling someone a "dag" (an affectionate term for someone unfashionable or quirky), are generally understood as good-natured but may require careful delivery to ensure they are received in the intended spirit.

It's also worth noting that some slang terms have a history or connotations that may not be immediately apparent. Words borrowed from Indigenous languages or other cultural groups, for example, should be used with respect and awareness of their origins. Understanding the cultural context behind these terms helps to avoid unintended offense and fosters greater cultural appreciation.

Non-verbal cues, such as body language and facial expressions, often accompany slang usage and contribute to its overall meaning. A wink, a smile, or a relaxed posture can reinforce the playful or informal nature of a slang term, while a serious tone or stern expression may alter its interpretation. Paying attention to these cues helps ensure that your message is conveyed accurately and received positively.

Avoiding Misunderstandings

While slang can enrich communication, it also carries the potential for misunderstandings, particularly when used across cultural or linguistic boundaries. To avoid miscommunication, it's essential to be aware of the limitations and risks associated with slang and take proactive steps to minimize confusion.

One common source of misunderstanding is the assumption that everyone shares the same knowledge or understanding of slang terms. Even within Australia, slang usage can vary widely between regions, age groups, and social circles. A term that is widely understood in one state may be unfamiliar or carry a different meaning in another. For instance, "sanga" (sandwich) is commonly used in New South Wales but might not be as prevalent elsewhere. To avoid confusion, it's helpful to gauge your audience's familiarity with the slang you're using and provide clarification if needed.

Another challenge arises when slang terms are translated or interpreted by non-native speakers. Australian slang, with its unique idioms and expressions, can be particularly perplexing to those unfamiliar with the culture. For example, phrases like "flat out like a lizard drinking" (very busy) or "fair dinkum" (genuine or true) may be baffling to outsiders without proper context. When communicating with international audiences, consider providing explanations or avoiding highly localized slang to ensure your message is clear.

Ambiguity is another potential pitfall of slang usage. Many slang terms have multiple meanings or rely heavily on context for interpretation. The word "deadset," for example, can mean "seriously" or "genuine," depending on the situation. To minimize ambiguity, it's important to ensure that the context of your conversation provides enough clues for the intended meaning to be understood.

Avoiding stereotypes and clichés is also crucial when using slang, especially in cross-cultural communication. While slang can be a fun and engaging way to connect, overusing or relying solely on stereotypical expressions can come across as patronizing or inauthentic. Striking a balance between embracing local slang and maintaining natural conversation ensures that your communication feels genuine and respectful.

Finally, if a misunderstanding does occur, it's important to address it with humility and openness. If someone misinterprets your use of slang, take the opportunity to explain your intent and learn from the experience. This approach not only resolves the immediate issue but also deepens your understanding of the complexities of language and culture.

Glossary of Australian Slang Terms

Australian slang is a vibrant and dynamic aspect of the nation's linguistic identity, offering insights into its humor, culture, and way of life. This glossary serves as an extensive guide to understanding and using Australian slang effectively. It is structured with alphabetical listings of terms, accompanied by definitions, examples, and notes on their usage and variations. Whether you're a local looking to deepen your understanding or an outsider seeking to connect with Australian culture, this comprehensive glossary will provide clarity and context for a wide range of expressions.

Alphabetical Listing of Terms

Australian slang spans a diverse range of expressions, many of which have unique meanings and cultural significance. By organizing these terms alphabetically, this glossary ensures easy navigation and quick reference. Below is a selection of commonly used slang terms:

A

Arvo: Short for "afternoon." Example: "Let's catch up this arvo for coffee."

Aussie: A colloquial term for an Australian. Example: "Aussies love their footy and barbecues."

B

Barbie: Short for "barbecue." Example: "We're having a barbie on Sunday, bring some snags."

Bloke: A casual term for a man. Example: "He's a good bloke, always willing to help."

C

Chockers: Full to capacity. Example: "The bus was chockers this morning."

Cuppa: A cup of tea or coffee. Example: "Do you fancy a cuppa before we head out?"

D

Dag: An affectionate term for someone unfashionable or quirky. Example: "He's a bit of a dag but has a great sense of humor."

Drongo: A foolish or clumsy person. Example: "Don't be a drongo; read the instructions first."

E

Esky: A portable cooler. Example: "Bring the esky; we'll need it for the drinks."

F

Fair dinkum: Genuine or true. Example: "Is that story fair dinkum, or are you pulling my leg?"

Flat out: Very busy. Example: "I've been flat out all day at work."

G

G'day: A friendly greeting meaning "hello." Example: "G'day, mate! How's it going?"

Groggy: Tired or unsteady. Example: "I felt a bit groggy after the late-night party."

H

Hooroo: A casual way to say "goodbye." Example: "Hooroo! See you tomorrow."

I

Icy pole: A popsicle or ice lolly. Example: "The kids had icy poles to cool down on the hot day."

J

Jumper: A sweater. Example: "It's chilly outside; don't forget your jumper."

K

Knackered: Extremely tired. Example: "After the hike, we were all knackered."

L

Larrikin: A playful, mischievous person. Example: "He's a real larrikin, always cracking jokes."

M

Mate: A term for a friend or companion. Example: "Thanks for helping out, mate."

Mozzie: A mosquito. Example: "Better bring some spray; the mozzies are everywhere."

N

No worries: A phrase meaning "it's okay" or "don't worry about it." Example: "Thanks for your help!" "No worries!"

O

Outback: Remote and rural areas of Australia. Example: "They live in the outback, far from the city."

P

Petrol: Gasoline or fuel. Example: "We need to stop for petrol before we head out."

Prezzy: A gift or present. Example: "I got a little prezzy for your birthday."

R

Ripper: Excellent or great. Example: "That was a ripper game of footy!"

Rubbish: Garbage or trash. Example: "Can you take out the rubbish, please?"

S

Servo: A service station or gas station. Example: "Let's stop at the servo to grab some snacks."

Straya: A colloquial way of saying "Australia." Example: "Straya's beaches are the best in the world."

T

Tucker: Food or a meal. Example: "What's for tucker tonight?"

U

Ute: A utility vehicle or pickup truck. Example: "We loaded the tools into the ute."

W

Whinge: To complain or whine. Example: "Stop whingeing and just get it done."

Y

Yakka: Hard work. Example: "It's going to take a lot of yakka to finish this project."

Z

Zonked: Extremely tired or exhausted. Example: "After a long day, I was completely zonked."

Definitions and Examples

Providing clear definitions and examples helps to clarify the meaning of each term and how it is used in everyday conversations. Australian slang is often descriptive and playful, reflecting the humor and creativity of the culture. Each term in this glossary is accompanied by an example sentence to demonstrate its usage in context.

For instance, "arvo" is a widely used abbreviation for "afternoon." It reflects Australians' tendency to shorten words while maintaining clarity. Example: "I'll meet you this arvo to go over the plans." Similarly, "fair dinkum" is a versatile phrase that can mean "genuine," "authentic," or "truthful," depending on the context. Example: "He's a fair dinkum Aussie who loves the outback."

By incorporating examples, this glossary not only explains the meaning of each term but also provides readers with practical insights into how to use them naturally.

Notes on Usage and Variations

Australian slang is deeply influenced by regional differences, cultural history, and social contexts. Many terms have variations in usage or meaning depending on the state or territory, the age group using them, or the specific social setting.

For example, the term "bathers" (swimwear) is commonly used in Victoria, while "togs" is more prevalent in Queensland. Understanding these regional variations can help users adapt their language to different parts of Australia and avoid confusion.

The influence of Indigenous languages on Australian slang is another important aspect to consider. Words like "boomerang" and "kangaroo" are derived from Indigenous languages and have become integral to Australian English. Respecting the origins and cultural significance of these terms is essential when using them in conversation.

Social context also plays a role in the acceptability of certain slang terms. Playful insults, such as "drongo" or "dag," are often used among friends as terms of endearment but can be misunderstood if used in a formal or unfamiliar setting. Similarly, terms like "mate" are commonly used to address strangers in casual interactions, but their tone and delivery can influence how they are perceived.

Australian slang is also evolving, with new terms emerging from social media, pop culture, and international influences. For example, phrases like "binge-watching" or "selfie" have been adopted into Australian vernacular, reflecting global linguistic trends. Keeping up with these changes ensures that language remains relevant and relatable.

www.ingramcontent.com/pod-product-compliance
Lightning Source LLC
Chambersburg PA
CBHW050818250726
48653CB00006B/2298